This Journal belongs to:

_____

"One important key to success is self-confidence. An important key to self-confidence is preparation."
— Arthur Ashe

Introduction

This journal is designed to help you manage every one of your interviews. The more you interview, the better you become. Part of the process is preparation. Ideally, you would have researched the organization, dissected the job description, and knew exactly who you were meeting prior to the interview.

Inside you will find:

1. Interview tracking page – Track the organization, HR rep contact info, and interviewer contact information
2. Debriefing page – Critique how the interview went

Debriefing is important in order to learn from each experience and build your interviewing chops.

After each interview you should be able to answer the following questions:

- What went well?
    - What parts of the interview went well for you and/or the interviewer?
- What could have gone better?
    - What part of the interview did not go over so well (questions/responses/body language)?
- What will I do differently?
    - Consider the things you would expand upon that went well, adjust for what didn't go well, and identify things that should have been emphasized more.
- Next Steps:
    - This is where you document your next steps such as sending a thank you note, thinking about what needs to be done for the next round of interviews, etc.

This journal also applies to tracking informational interviews as you network. Utilize this journal to stay organized and on top of your game.

Interviewing

Interviewing takes practice. You must be prepared for both one on one and panel interviews (multiple interviewers in one session). The interview allows you to create a rapport with the interviewers to assess fit and demonstrate that you have the skills required for the role. Most interviewers utilize behavioral interview questions.

*Behavioral interview questions: questions designed to have the candidate share how they would respond to certain situations.

Hiring managers love these questions.

Depending on the role, these questions will most likely cover any one of the following:

- Motivation
- Communication
- Time Management
- Adaptability
- Client-Facing
- Teamwork

You should be prepared to answer all of these questions as it pertains to your work experience.

One framework that really helps in demonstrating a clear, concise response to these questions is the STAR method.

Star Method

- Situation: Set the scene
- Task: Your responsibility in the situation
- Action: Explain your process to resolve the situation
- Result: Describe the outcomes of your actions

The STAR method organizes your thoughts so they are concise and easily digestible for the interviewer.

Practice and Preparation are Key

Don't be afraid to practice with a friend or record yourself on your phone. Be methodical in your preparation to eliminate any self-doubt that you are the right person for this role.

Best of Luck!

Interview # _____

Organization Name: _____

Role: _____

HR Rep/Recruiter: _____

✉ Email: _____

📞 Phone: _____

Interviewer Name: _____

Position: _____

✉ Email: _____

📞 Phone: _____

Notes:

_____
_____
_____
_____
_____

What went well?

_____
_____
_____

What could have gone better?

_____
_____
_____

What will I do differently?

_____
_____
_____

Next Steps:

_____
_____
_____
_____

Interview # _____

Organization Name: _____

Role: _____

HR Rep/Recruiter: _____

✉ Email: _____

📞 Phone: _____

Interviewer Name: _____

Position: _____

✉ Email: _____

📞 Phone: _____

Notes:

_____
_____
_____
_____
_____

What went well?

_____
_____
_____

What could have gone better?

_____
_____
_____

What will I do differently?

_____
_____
_____

Next Steps:

_____
_____
_____
_____

Interview # _____

Organization Name: _____

Role: _____

HR Rep/Recruiter: _____

✉ Email: _____

☎ Phone: _____

Interviewer Name: _____

Position: _____

✉ Email: _____

☎ Phone: _____

Notes:

_____
_____
_____
_____
_____

Debrief

What went well?

_____
_____
_____

What could have gone better?

_____
_____
_____

What will I do differently?

_____
_____
_____

Next Steps:

Interview # _____

Organization Name: _____

Role: _____

HR Rep/Recruiter: _____

✉ Email: _____

📞 Phone: _____

Interviewer Name: _____

Position: _____

✉ Email: _____

📞 Phone: _____

Notes:

_____
_____
_____
_____
_____

Debrief

What went well?

_____
_____
_____

What could have gone better?

_____
_____
_____

What will I do differently?

_____
_____
_____

Next Steps:

Interview # _____

Organization Name: _____

Role: _____

HR Rep/Recruiter: _____

📧 Email: _____

📞 Phone: _____

Interviewer Name: _____

Position: _____

📧 Email: _____

📞 Phone: _____

Notes:

_____
_____
_____
_____
_____

What went well?

_____
_____
_____

What could have gone better?

_____
_____
_____

What will I do differently?

_____
_____
_____

Next Steps:

_____
_____
_____
_____
_____

Interview # _____

Organization Name: _____

Role: _____

HR Rep/Recruiter: _____

✉ Email: _____

☎ Phone: _____

Interviewer Name: _____

Position: _____

✉ Email: _____

☎ Phone: _____

Notes:

_____
_____
_____
_____
_____

What went well?

_____
_____
_____

What could have gone better?

_____
_____
_____

What will I do differently?

_____
_____
_____

Next Steps:

_____
_____
_____
_____

Interview # _____

Organization Name: _____

Role: _____

HR Rep/Recruiter: _____

✉ Email: _____

☎ Phone: _____

Interviewer Name: _____

Position: _____

✉ Email: _____

☎ Phone: _____

Notes:

_____
_____
_____
_____

Debrief

What went well?

_____
_____
_____

What could have gone better?

_____
_____
_____

What will I do differently?

_____
_____
_____

Next Steps:

_____
_____
_____
_____
_____

Interview # _____

Organization Name: _____

Role: _____

HR Rep/Recruiter: _____

@ Email: _____

☎ Phone: _____

Interviewer Name: _____

Position: _____

@ Email: _____

☎ Phone: _____

Notes:

_____
_____
_____
_____
_____

What went well?

_____
_____
_____

What could have gone better?

_____
_____
_____

What will I do differently?

_____
_____
_____

Next Steps:

_____
_____
_____
_____
_____

Interview # _____

Organization Name: _____

Role: _____

HR Rep/Recruiter: _____

✉ **Email:** _____

📞 **Phone:** _____

Interviewer Name: _____

Position: _____

✉ **Email:** _____

📞 **Phone:** _____

Notes:

_____
_____
_____
_____
_____

What went well?

_____
_____
_____

What could have gone better?

_____
_____
_____

What will I do differently?

_____
_____
_____

Next Steps:

_____
_____
_____
_____

Interview # _____

Organization Name: _____

Role: _____

HR Rep/Recruiter: _____

Email: _____

Phone: _____

Interviewer Name: _____

Position: _____

Email: _____

Phone: _____

Notes:

_____

_____

_____

_____

_____

What went well?

_____
_____
_____

What could have gone better?

_____
_____
_____

What will I do differently?

_____
_____
_____

Next Steps:

_____
_____
_____
_____
_____

Interview # _____

Organization Name: _____

Role: _____

HR Rep/Recruiter: _____

✉ Email: _____

📞 Phone: _____

Interviewer Name: _____

Position: _____

✉ Email: _____

📞 Phone: _____

Notes:

_____
_____
_____
_____
_____

Debrief

What went well?

_____
_____
_____

What could have gone better?

_____
_____
_____

What will I do differently?

_____
_____
_____

Next Steps:

_____
_____
_____
_____
_____

Interview # _____

Organization Name: _____

Role: _____

HR Rep/Recruiter: _____

✉ Email: _____

☏ Phone: _____

Interviewer Name: _____

Position: _____

✉ Email: _____

☏ Phone: _____

Notes:

_____
_____
_____
_____
_____

What went well?

___

What could have gone better?

___

What will I do differently?

___

Next Steps:

Interview # _____

Organization Name: _____

Role: _____

HR Rep/Recruiter: _____

@ Email: _____

📞 Phone: _____

Interviewer Name: _____

Position: _____

@ Email: _____

📞 Phone: _____

Notes:

_____
_____
_____
_____
_____

What went well?

_____
_____
_____

What could have gone better?

_____
_____
_____

What will I do differently?

_____
_____
_____

Next Steps:

_____
_____
_____
_____

Interview # _____

Organization Name: _____

Role: _____

HR Rep/Recruiter: _____

📧 Email: _____

📞 Phone: _____

Interviewer Name: _____

Position: _____

📧 Email: _____

📞 Phone: _____

Notes:

_____
_____
_____
_____
_____

What went well?

_____
_____
_____

What could have gone better?

_____
_____
_____

What will I do differently?

_____
_____
_____

Next Steps:

_____
_____
_____
_____

Interview # _____

Organization Name: _____

Role: _____

HR Rep/Recruiter: _____

@ Email: _____

☏ Phone: _____

Interviewer Name: _____

Position: _____

@ Email: _____

☏ Phone: _____

Notes:

_____
_____
_____
_____
_____

What went well?

_____
_____
_____

What could have gone better?

_____
_____
_____

What will I do differently?

_____
_____
_____

Next Steps:

_____
_____
_____
_____
_____

Interview # _____

Organization Name: _____

Role: _____

HR Rep/Recruiter: _____

✉ Email: _____

📞 Phone: _____

Interviewer Name: _____

Position: _____

✉ Email: _____

📞 Phone: _____

Notes:

_____
_____
_____
_____
_____

What went well?

_____
_____
_____

What could have gone better?

_____
_____
_____

What will I do differently?

_____
_____
_____

Next Steps:

_____
_____
_____
_____
_____

Interview # _____

Organization Name: _____

Role: _____

HR Rep/Recruiter: _____

✉ Email: _____

📞 Phone: _____

Interviewer Name: _____

Position: _____

✉ Email: _____

📞 Phone: _____

Notes:

_____

_____

_____

_____

What went well?

_____
_____
_____

What could have gone better?

_____
_____
_____

What will I do differently?

_____
_____
_____

Next Steps:

_____
_____
_____
_____
_____

Interview # _____

Organization Name: _____

Role: _____

HR Rep/Recruiter: _____

✉ Email: _____

📞 Phone: _____

Interviewer Name: _____

Position: _____

✉ Email: _____

📞 Phone: _____

Notes:

_____
_____
_____
_____
_____

What went well?

_____
_____
_____

What could have gone better?

_____
_____
_____

What will I do differently?

_____
_____
_____

Next Steps:

_____
_____
_____
_____

Interview # _____

Organization Name: _____

Role: _____

HR Rep/Recruiter: _____

✉ **Email:** _____

📞 **Phone:** _____

Interviewer Name: _____

Position: _____

✉ **Email:** _____

📞 **Phone:** _____

Notes:

_____

_____

_____

_____

_____

Debrief

What went well?

_____
_____
_____

What could have gone better?

_____
_____
_____

What will I do differently?

_____
_____
_____

Next Steps:

_____
_____
_____
_____

Interview # _____

Organization Name: _____

Role: _____

HR Rep/Recruiter: _____

✉ Email: _____

📞 Phone: _____

Interviewer Name: _____

Position: _____

✉ Email: _____

📞 Phone: _____

Notes:

_____
_____
_____
_____
_____

What went well?

_____

_____

_____

What could have gone better?

_____

_____

_____

What will I do differently?

_____

_____

_____

Next Steps:

_____

_____

_____

_____

_____

Interview # _____

Organization Name: _____

Role: _____

HR Rep/Recruiter: _____

Email: _____

Phone: _____

Interviewer Name: _____

Position: _____

Email: _____

Phone: _____

Notes:

_____
_____
_____
_____
_____

What went well?

_____
_____
_____

What could have gone better?

_____
_____
_____

What will I do differently?

_____
_____
_____

Next Steps:

_____
_____
_____
_____
_____

Interview # _____

Organization Name: _____

Role: _____

HR Rep/Recruiter: _____

✉ Email: _____

📞 Phone: _____

Interviewer Name: _____

Position: _____

✉ Email: _____

📞 Phone: _____

Notes:

_____
_____
_____
_____
_____

Debrief

What went well?

_____
_____
_____

What could have gone better?

_____
_____
_____

What will I do differently?

_____
_____
_____

Next Steps:

_____
_____
_____
_____
_____

Interview # _____

Organization Name: _____

Role: _____

HR Rep/Recruiter: _____

@ Email: _____

📞 Phone: _____

Interviewer Name: _____

Position: _____

@ Email: _____

📞 Phone: _____

Notes:

_____
_____
_____
_____
_____

What went well?

_____
_____
_____

What could have gone better?

_____
_____
_____

What will I do differently?

_____
_____
_____

Next Steps:

_____
_____
_____
_____
_____

Interview # _____

Organization Name: _____

Role: _____

HR Rep/Recruiter: _____

✉ Email: _____

📞 Phone: _____

Interviewer Name: _____

Position: _____

✉ Email: _____

📞 Phone: _____

Notes:

_____
_____
_____
_____
_____

Debrief

What went well?

_____

_____

_____

What could have gone better?

_____

_____

_____

What will I do differently?

_____

_____

_____

Next Steps:

_____

_____

_____

_____

_____

www.ingramcontent.com/pod-product-compliance
Lightning Source LLC
Chambersburg PA
CBHW061345040426
42444CB00011B/3096